Advance Praise for *Vessels*

A late addition to the great tradition of wisdom texts, Robert van Vliet's VESSELS attends to what it means to be alive in the anthropocene, an era of climate destruction and dislocation from the natural world. "That is / the puzzle for / every generation," he poses, "to / fix what has / been fixed." The poet's gentle, prophetic voice ekes out an intrepid authority, half-whispered into the ear as "water whispers to / the seed as it lies / on its belly," and the poems function as both meditations and instructions for use. "Speak / carefully," he instructs in one of the book's many near-adages, "or the / listening fish will mistake / your confusion for their order." Guided by gnostic and transcendentalist thought and built on found materials and chance operations, these poems walk a wooded path, where there is refuge, dissonance, ash, strange magic, and where below the observable world is the "unforeseen" territory of the spirit.

— Jane Huffman, author of *Public Abstract*

Written—composed—assembled—or *made*, through processes both of aleatory and of careful composition, over the course of a moment of profound historical, social, and existential angst, the poems of Robert van Vliet's VESSELS are marvelous, echoing, delicate crystals of profound stillness. They resonate with wisdom—the vivid metaphors of the *I Ching*, Thoreau's quotidian observations, ancient Gnosis. But these vessels of stillness shiver with the promise of both revelation and obliteration, leaving the reader moved and disquieted by van Vliet's subtle lyric art.

— Mark Scroggins, author of *Zion Offramp 1-50*

In VESSELS, Robert van Vliet works as a medium, reminding us that foundational texts—in this case the *I Ching*, Thoreau's writings, and the Nag Hammadi library—can constitute us as much as the news cycle. Here, past fortitude and present urgency scrape against each other like tectonic plates. In the tradition of such wisdom literature, van Vliet's poems are koan-like, gnomic, paradoxical, shot through with uncertainty and stitched together with guesswork. But they are also unmistakably tangible: van Vliet shuffles the natural world and fans its elements before us like tarot cards—"a flat cloud stained like a bloody liver"; "a nest of hair above the dry lake"; "thunder swim[ming] over the mountains." The subject matter of VESSELS is nothing less than the act of poetic creation. Van Vliet invites us to consider how and why we make poetry, and how we might use it to survive these times.

—Claire Wahmanholm, author of *Meltwater*

"The sky remembers / what the tongue / can no longer pronounce" because the world, as well, is a vessel. Its containment may not be discernible because the world is vast. But world—like its word itself—holds all within its embrace. Such poses necessary implications, like "the hope of forgiveness" or like how one "work[s] on what / has been spoiled, not / dwelling too much on // who spoiled it and / why." All creatures, such as humans, are also vessels but because we're all within the same world, when we hear others as "the red / clay cracking in the empty lake. /...we must / help each other." To live in a shared vessel also means the relevance of courage: "the tree is more than its reach." Robert van Vliet's VESSELS is not only moving and engaging poetry; its words also have crafted a worthwhile lesson that can be summed up by the book's beautiful raison d'etre: "Every straight line / is perfectly round."

—Eileen R. Tabios, author of *THE INVENTOR: A Poet's*
Transcolonial Autobiography

Robert van Vliet's poems are, paradoxically, bth quiet and powerful. With an understated idiom, they express remorse, unease, and struggle – while delivering, at the end, a sense of enigmatic wonder and peace. It is a balance of contraries. The poems are forthright, simple and clear: yet beneath their unobtrusive surface resides a well of glowing, flashing images; an urge toward existential reckoning. Simone Weil wrote: *Absolutely unmixed attention is prayer. If we turn our mind toward the good, it is impossible that little by little the whole soul will not be attracted thereto in spite of itself.* The challenging, obdurate, questing voice at the heart of VESSELS is unmistakably authentic. It unfolds a basic sense of rightness – which offers, to the reader, a profound encounter with reality.

—Henry Gould, author of *The Green Radius*

VESSELS is a spiritual text, a canticle, but not necessarily a denominational one. A catechism in the sense it is an exposition of belief, where the mysteries of nature & relationships are the divinities. It is a communion with oneself, with others, with the great beyond. It is a thoughtful & thought-provoking compendium of answers to those questions we needed someone more astute than ourselves to ask.

—Mark Young

The poems in Robert van Vliet's debut collection murmur with quiet affirmations of being-in-the-world; the sounds the earth makes when no one is listening but which, nevertheless, pulse with fragile urgency.

To swim over the green
earth, as thunder swims
over the mountains. And we

will meet beneath the lake, to
drink in readiness.

VESSELS performs a book-length meditation on evanescence and the deep pleasures of the immediate. The reader who surrenders to these richly enigmatic poems will find themselves floating inside the aviaries of Logos, ready to embrace the gifts of spirit.

—Patrick Pritchett

Language is both the landscape of meaning in which we live and a tool for exploring, shaping, and reshaping that landscape. Rooted in operations that make use of both those truths, the poems in Robert van Vliet's VESSELS illuminate with a laser-sharp clarity the path one consciousness has taken in order to build, moment of perception by moment of perception, a meaning for his life. It's a path well worth walking with him. You will learn important lessons about what it takes and what it feels like to make that journey for yourself.

—Richard Jeffrey Newman, author of *T'shuvah*

Vessels

Robert van Vliet

For information contact:
Unsolicited Press
Portland, Oregon
www.unsolicitedpress.com
orders@unsolicitedpress.com
619-354-8005

Front Cover Design: Kathryn Gerhardt
Editor: S.R. Stewart

ISBN: 978-1-956692-89-1

In Zen they say:
   If something is boring after two minutes,
      try it for four.
   If still boring,
      try it for eight, sixteen,
      thirty-two, and so on.

Eventually one discovers
   it's not boring at all
   but very interesting.

—John Cage

You must ask, Why this song, this seeing.

—Dana Levin

Vessels

I

This Folded Path

Guard the Mysteries!
Constantly reveal them!

—Lew Welch

that is that is not

       this
   this
this
       stop
   running
 this

is the only way

       dogs
     riverbeds
  escape
       kindness
     perfect thought
 peace
       repose
   weariness
 the mountain
      the weather
   memory
 reason

you long for more
because praying will not help
burn it burn the smallest prayers
every night and say
you will want to wait
for each

                    eye
          hand

hair like

                        floods
                green light
          fingers

                over you

you

1

The
gentle wind
above the houses.

Everything that is
new is
not

new.
Heaven creates
itself without doing

anything. A long
river like
a

claw.
A flat
cloud stained like

a bloody liver.
What else
but

this
can any
of it mean?

2

Fire in the lake and
clouds of ash. The heavens
are within the mountain
just as wisdom listens
from within the ancient
water. Seeds return
to roots, return to seeds.

3

To swim over the green
earth, as thunder swims
over the mountains. And we

will meet beneath the lake, to
drink in readiness. It is in
such gatherings, in reverence

and in grief, that we meet
the unforeseen. And together
we will walk the round

road until the few
seem to be the ten
thousand things.

4

Tell me:
what do you
mean by good?

Lying on warm grass?
Forgiveness and fire?
A woman caught
in thunder and rain?

The tail knows
what the head guesses.

5

That which is bright rises twice: once
through blood, once through
the four lit corners
of the world. It is good
to die by a window looking out
upon the distant law. Where
there were two there is now
only fire—thunder
and no lightning, lightning
and no cloud.

6

As new bone
stitches itself with
time, we must
sit with our
ears to the
gentle wind, listening
to the red
clay cracking in
the empty lake.
And we must
help each other.

7

Thwart evil, nurture goodness.

This is easy to say
but difficult to do,
like drawing a bird

from a stone. But

the sky remembers
what the tongue
can no longer pronounce.

everything true was once confused

the moon
beyond this false dawn

is it possible you
        never thought the clouds can walk away
it will not come
        by filling the sky with smoke
it is not enough to owe
        what the tongue cannot say

memory makes death as long as love
        its reflection in the wind

we had nothing
to say and he said only
that it was his own flesh

and we still believe after so much

she said I will have the same answer for you
over this fine anger
I loved only the hope of forgiveness
beyond the bloodless moon
I asked for peace and
lost my way

8

You work on what
has been spoiled, not
dwelling too much on

who spoiled it and
why. They tore up
the roots, you plant

a new tree. The
watchful eye is on
you and on them.

You do not know
what is to come,
but neither do they.

Like a horn blowing
low over the mountains.
Slow destruction. Slow healing.

9

Is it enough to sit, keeping
still, as the mountains
stand so close together?

Is it enough to wish the rain
would rise again from
the earth? And is it

enough to receive the earth
just as it is: leaning
its head against
the green clouds?

10

A long road made longer:
walking back and forth.
A mouth that can't stop
singing. A cloud that
never cries. Thunder
always rolling over
the empty lake.

A long road made longer:
walking up and down.
Restless as fire. Blank
as the full moon.
Never standing still.
Never standing firm.

11

Even as the small
departs, the great approaches.
Can you recognize it?
So easy to recline
when lying is called
for. This is not
the same as persevering.
The light has sunk
into the earth. Deep
in its bones, we
can still shine. And
peace still has a
bite. You cannot receive
if you cannot give.

12

This cold summer
of interruptions, this
persistence, this motley
answer, this green misfortune,
this lonely person starting out
too late, this folded path,
this blank rain which has
already forgotten
all the names for water.

13

As lions' teeth smile
with their own joyous secrets,
at last you give up waiting
for riches to rain down on you.

And as the moon has turned
her back on the lake, you know
in your skin that this
is the wrong path.

14

The wind drives the clouds

across heaven.
You are like a seed

returning to the way.
This small movement

is full of a taming power.
Your skin guesses

what your belly knows.

will they wonder how to name
the stone seeking to hunt them
under the pitiless sun

when bones became soft voices again
every star sent
its own question

and ash endures longer
than you the sky the sun the night the sand

bolt your doors
wait for the dust
keep from weeping without hope

the future will have to satisfy you
where you will soon be erased

the sun   the sun

an argument
in the cloud
like a mask

15

Two choices but each
choice is many. This is why
the beginning is always

so difficult. So speak
carefully, or the
listening fish will mistake
your confusion for their order.

16

You only walk
the known and
well-ordered paths.
And this is
what you wait
for, and this
is what you
listen for, as
you walk: this
moment when a
new name rises
like twilight spoken
by the dusk.
And the sand
listens to the
tide as a
feather hears the
winds, one following
after the other.

17

The mountain rests
on the earth.
The tree is more
than its reach.
You can listen
even as you kneel.
Undertake small things.
Give generously.
Do not go anywhere.
There is blood on the path
and fire at the foot
of the mountain.

18

Have you forgotten that even
bone can be killed,
buried in a nest
of hair above the dry lake?

Have you forgotten that the moon
longs to die
in the deep water,
a mountain within the earth
like yolk within an egg?

19

Who can tell you
what you don't

want to hear? Who
can tell you

which path brought you
here? The path

glaring white in the
moonlight, the path

red with fallen maple
leaves, the path

over the mountain,
the path under the

lake, or the path
slick with blood?

20

A wood fire. The sun
following a cloud
like an obedient dog.

It is a small thing: wait
three days, then
wait three more.

You gain by giving.
Every straight line
is perfectly round.

21

Each morning, more new leaves
like smoke in the branches.
Each midnight, setting your life
in order, examining your self
from the middle of the lake.
Waiting for thunder like a stone,
its ripples running outward
in rounds forever.

II

This False Life

Even the wisest and best are apt to use their lives as the occasion to do something else in than to live greatly. But we should hang as fondly over this work as the finishing and embellishment of a poem.

It is a great relief when for a few moments in the day we can retire to our chamber and be completely true to ourselves. It leavens the rest of our hours. In that moment I will be nakedly as vicious as I am; this false life of mine shall have a being at length.

—Thoreau, *Journal*

wonder
wind
tree
table
crown
place

it was too hot to believe the cold
night the right answer

flesh
reason
will throw the song
and the silence will hide from you
never asking why
peace is for everyone

the sun   the sun
they will wait

you weep and stand on this parched root
before a train of dust
always above you

and you sit as you always do

sand
moon
syllable

29 August

Because I did not know its name
I could not say how long this melody
had been in my head.

I did not know if it was true
or a fragment I had dreamed up.

As I walked up main street
I sang quietly but
there was no one in the neighborhood
who could tell me
what I needed to learn.

1 November

6:30am. This muddy path
beneath the early clouds,
delicate as fish bones.
Leaves, bright with surprise,
their red tongues gossiping.

To Hubbard's Bridge
to see the gossamer.

23 May

Blue sky! We wear it
as a bird wears
its song. Even when we
have heard its note
and looked for it
in vain. The horizon
throws itself over us
—so big it fits in
our pocket, so small
we buckle under its weight.

28 October

I am waiting for the ash
to stop falling. I am waiting
until the earth surprises me
with its new name. As I am
waiting, dawn throws a veil
over the last star, and I see
a screech owl sitting on the edge
of a hollow hemlock stump.

21 May

In this strange
outlandish world, so
barren, so raveled,
we think the
mysteries are more
interesting than the
solutions. We trip
over things in
the dark. We
are like fish
trying to stand.

11 September

Black vines screen
you from the
worst of it.
Something good comes
from the greatest
cataclysms. That is
the puzzle for
every generation: to
fix what has
been fixed. Every
winter, we wonder:
How much farther
is it back
to frost, again
and again, broken
anew each time?

5 December

The tree, a bare staff, wears its song
carefully like a reflection
of the snow tripping down
its tempered branches, around
a quarter of the way
up to the zenith.

14 March

When they said that everything must
die, where did you go? You crawled
under the foundation, hiding like a bug
bite, trying to ignore how the weather
painted you with its red impatience.
Like a new door ready to give birth,
the darkness refused to change
the subject. Darkness opened into
darkness, where at last you found
luminous traces of the old door. How else
did you expect it would end?

you told me we desire
sleep I remember
        the absent clouds
    the unhatched suns
under you

    you

you want to fight someone else's prayer

there it is

            I am green
        I am sun
        I am shadow

don't ask
how many more winters
I know what we
would forget

            the dead
        the hours
    the road
            the cold

like a moon and the dream
of your yellow dawn

and to let go of
        everything

20 October

What can a woman find in this dry place?
Can she find peace buried like a pebble in the sand?
Can she know frost if she cannot remember water?
Can she stand with her back to the caressing wind
and whisper "What a wild and rich domain"?

28 November

You hope each morning that
every place beneath the sun
is true—even anger, which

you visit like a favorite
motel. Bags of ice by the office.
Color TV. Swimming pool.

Beyond the highway, you watch
as the farmers are beginning
to pick up their dead wood.

11 June

Two yards of politeness do not make
society for me. Instead, I will ask you
to walk with me, listening
to your ten thousand names
for smoke. I will ask how you cleave
to your ancestors. You will tell me
the sun dies every evening, and
together we will sing of its trip
through our future to emerge
reborn at dawn. There is no harmony
without dissonance.

31 October

The air is dry only because
you believe that weather
could never be so cruel,
even after summer seduced you
in an unknown tongue.
You knew everything it said
was false, but you had nowhere else
to turn for help. Winter is a trap
covered with withered leaves.

1 August

The world will
stand round but
will not wait for you. It is not

enough
for you to follow your
nose if you do not know

the species of sedges and
grasses. Even the egg
is bound by

the true and will laugh
at your
intuition.

Tomorrow's guess grows
from
yesterday's lesson.

23 October

It was that time of summer
when we would eat like sleepwalkers,
languorously reading the braille
of twilight. We could not determine
if the sunset spoke like a woman
weary of interruptions or
like an egg waiting for ice water.
Only yesterday the sand in my
palm had been a mountain range
between us. Now everything seemed
so new. I never saw such colors
painted: each grain its own voice.
They were without spot.
Can we ever forgive ourselves?

25 August

He said the last good
night was about
forty years ago.
Too many since then—

Too many days, he said.
I asked him how
he knew. I asked him
how anyone could

explain. He said that
it is good when there
is nothing left to give,
when nothing else remains.

16 October

If you are afraid to ask, it is because
you know the answer you already
fear. This is not a small thing. "—by
his own hand." His hand. His hand
was nearby. He was tired of every
fight that doesn't seem like a fight
until the fighting starts. He kept telling
everyone: *white is a color, too.* But
the universe is made of stories,
not colors. He said, *I will walk upriver.*
I will listen to the current. I am
satisfied to live on fish alone
for a season.

the red   the white
what does this mean

you must look out
every leaf   every fish

because the first day will
erase the light and
*   they will*
turn away from
the chaos between night and day

*   I will not give way*
*   to sand*
pavement

*   I am*
*   I am*
he said
know your own heart
you are their black song
this is how they want this fear
*   open to the sky*
*   standing near the stones*

peace is nothing like love
terror is hiding you

*   you*
*   you*

I am and
        I am
    and I am
                with you everywhere

        I am
    here and I am
        not here

and the moon
and the sun

5 July

No matter how many times I asked,
the instructions were no help. So I stood
by the window, watching the buses pass,
all bound for parking lots as empty
as a table after the eviction.

And as the day began, I could still see
some stars, as surprising as
catching a handful of small
water-bugs skating on a lake of ash.

18 October

As yellow as a faint shadow,
a tall ribbon hanging
from the moon.

Seeds for spring, flies
for summer, tupelo for
autumn, and for winter
evergreen. The tail whispers
as the skin sleeps.

27 June

Works go steadily forward,
one cold whisper after another.
But I will have nothing to do.
Before me is a seed
as big as a moon.
A lifeless beginning,
as sanguine as a myth
waiting to be understood.
There is nothing
to do, and I will do it.

17 May

The smoke is dirty brown,
very nearly the color of the sky.

You cannot quite tell
the difference between
tooth and skin, meadow

and moat. You struggle
with anything that sounds
like a word, and you are afraid

to ask if the stones
can form sentences
as well as walls.

14 July

I spoke of good and evil like neighbors
or roommates. I would see them come and go,
always late for their appointments, never
stopping to chat, always with a smirk
in the corner of their mouth, always
in the know. I was new and it took me years
to fall through the blind suburban syllable
which was then but another name
for the extended world for me.

21 October

The tall grasses, sensitive
as the fine hair on your arm,
stand silently, offering no solace
and giving no advice. You can
say anything to them, and they
will keep your secret. With mud
on your knee, you perform
sacrament and purification.

16 November

The water whispers to
the seed as it lies
on its belly in the cold
morning. Like me, it is waiting
for that sudden bolt of joy
when you know you have
once again evaded
death. For the most part,
and I do not know why,
the universe is unaccountably
kind to me.

19 March

Is it something in the skin,
is it something within the dry
voice we hear as the fire
steps quietly along with us
as we go from song to song,
from dream to dream? Is it in
the ancient and unexhausted
energies of this new country?

III

This Empty Tongue

The soul
is something like a basin of water
and the sense impressions
are something like a ray of light
that falls upon the water

Now when the water moves
it looks like the ray of light moves too

But it does not move

— Epictetus

the puzzle again and again
hiding ready
the darkness traces the sand

a wild twilight
for yesterday such colors

you believe that was false
for me you emerge reborn

     for you
    for you
will laugh but refuse
waving and how still
its whole story

this is not a small thing

he said I will walk struggle
I asked him how anyone could hope
impossible river
so small

I asked the lake
     for summer
    for autumn
after another myth
but offering no solace

the horizon like
every broken voice we hear

1

I keep the day on my left

I remember that everything true
    was once untrue

I remember how you told me
    that whatever we desire
    we must say with reason

I remember how I once confused
    a mountain for the last hour of sleep

I remember I am
    in the process of becoming

2

what you hear
is a dog
pawing at the sand

when the moon snaps
like a cheap buckle
and the sky opens

nothing
covered will remain
without being
uncovered

3

Beyond this false dawn,
devoured by the absent
clouds, under this empty
tongue, and this heart
with no mouth, struggling
to see—how is it possible
these miserable ones
have no name?

4

Let the unhatched egg teach you
what to say.

Let the narrow street lead you
where you never thought to go.

Let the twelve suns come
into being under the temple.

5

What seems black to the eye
might simply be another
bird and we stand
waiting as our future
slowly drinks the sun

(and *future* has been corrected
by a later hand to *torture*)

6

It will not come by waiting for it.
Does this anger you? Do you
want to fight against the implications?
It is not like the dawn filling
the sky with yellow smoke: that
is someone else's prayer, burning
like flesh every morning. And you
cannot simply call it to you.
It is not a matter of saying
Here it is or *There it is.*
You must build it, and
you must build it again.

the worst of it
every winter

can a woman stand
with summer when weary

can we ever forgive you
winter is a trap

walk with me
every evening together

> *without the world*
> > *the sedges and*
> > > *yesterday's forest*

walk upward
you are afraid to ask
because to live alone
between the stones
there is nothing left

you are beginning
> *to help*
> *the water*
the birds
> *as big as a moon*

I spoke of never stopping to fall
the grasses will keep your secret

even in our vigilance
from song to dream

7

How can it have been so long? A year
for every foot, a foot for every loss.
Grown mean after so much heartbreak.
How the hours wear you down. A doorstep
that has never known peace. Say your name,
she said, so that I may show you the road.

8

Don't ask what your heart
doesn't want to know:
Is this a false memory?
And what makes death false?
And how many more winters
until we can't remember
the cold? Your heart lives
within you only as long
as you love her and never
interrogate her. Before you
were born, she came to this world,
which is all the night sees
when it gazes at its reflection
in the still pond.

9

A wind that blasts the bark
off trees, that drives the water
standing behind everything.
A wind that reminds us
we will die, and at last all who
are unnumbered will have been named.

10

"What would you give to take it
all back?" He had nothing to say
to that. He only scratched
the back of his neck slowly,
pretending to think. And the sky
bloomed slowly. And he said only
that it was a very fine evening. But
I know that he struggled against
passions—and condemned their
error—as though they were his own.

11

The flesh teaches us what we would forget,
what we would never want to know:
that the heart is a foundering ship,
its cargo contraband. Waiting
on the rocks, a whisper lost
beneath the rain and wind,
waiting for the tide to return
what the tide stole. And we still
believe that he rose from the dead.

12

No repose can cure
    your weariness.
For this reason, she is held
    to have said:

I am green and
I am what is not green

I am the tongue and
I am what the tongue cannot say

I am the sun and
I am the sun's shadow.

And whenever you appear, I will hide from you.

the wind like a claw
the heavens swim
over the earth such gatherings seem
to be caught in
        the thunder
     the fire
   the wind

this is no longer a new tree
low so close it is leaning
against a cloud
blank as the full moon
so easy in its bones

this persistence this
blank rain at last you
give up the wrong movement
so difficult and well-ordered

a new name rises
after the small things forget

       deep water
     the path
   the lake

      wait
   new
 new
leaves like a stone

this melody I sang
beneath the water of joy

you know by seeking

discovery
I am waiting

> *the tree*
the way

13

On some windblown afternoon, you
go to temple. Ask anyone you meet. They
will all have the same answer for you. He
is ineffable since no one
is able to comprehend him
enough to speak of him.

14

Water flows around him
  like sleep wearing a hole
  in itself.

The cold passes him without
  a word, like lovers years
  before they meet.

Do not puzzle over this
  too long—for what name
  is given to him
  who does not exist?

15

Because I trusted you
with all my strength, I thought it fine
to swallow my anger like a moon, sit

motionless as you threw acid
and daggers at everything
I thought I loved, until I loved

only the hope of trust
and the dream of you
at last dissolving

your daggers in the acid,
and together we would watch
the sun rise like forgiveness.

16

Beyond the yellow dawn
as it devours the last
of yesterday's noon,
still asleep under the long
bloodless moon, I asked
for peace and you gave me
a cold and inverted fire.
And because your grace
is alive in me, I have never
lost my way among
the last embers.

17

We called that fish his glory because he had nothing else.
The child of the child had to die for his ear to hear anything.
This is what it means to let go of everything.

18

On this ship that is no ship,
as it founders on the rocks that are not rocks,
the passengers wonder: Will he comfort everyone?

And they stumble over soil that is not soil,
past trees without roots.
As the wind that is not wind bites at them, they wonder:
How is it proper to cause anyone such discomfort?

everything is new
what else

wisdom listens over the mountains
and we meet
tell me

> *what*
what

the world

> *lightning*
lightning

red clay to say you work on what is on you

> *slow*
slow

rain clouds

a long road always rolling
standing still

when this still has this green rain
and as the wind drives your skin
so carefully and

this is spoken by

the dusk
the mountains
the earth

buried within the moonlight the path
wait you gain each midnight

its ripples in my head
in the leaves

for the last star
like a reflection

19

How the leaf cannot remember the tree
How the table cannot name the stone

How many times
How much contention

This is false
This is not false
This is the crown
This is the great

20

They hunt, sleepless,
seeking out, among the liminal
and the vigilant, those
who long
to stop running.
There is no place for you
in their reckoning. If you turn
to hunt them—feather,
fast blood, surprise on
the snow—this is the only
way your redemption
will be preserved from them.

21

Footsore under the pitiless
sun, lost like dogs
crossing parched riverbeds,
we staggered on until
it was too hot to believe
anything anymore, when
our bones became vaporous
and sought to escape
through the smoke hole
at the tops of our skulls.
Wavering there in the mirage,
soft voices caressed us
and they showed great
kindness toward us . . .

22

In order that the cold
should not come again
but there should be
the unity of perfect thought,
they gathered in the blushing
night to audition the right
answer: that every star
is only red dust
sent to smother dissent.

23

To keep the peace, they said. And
they beat him, all but killing
him. Flesh is its own answer, but
the night is its own question.

24

Sorrow endures longer than
    memory.
For this reason she is held
    to have said:

I am the tree and
I am the cleansing ash
    it yearns for

I am the mountain and
I am the weather
    that will throw it down.

heaven creates fire within water
we will meet the unforeseen together

good night
the distant bone
the empty lake

a bird
a stone

too much not enough
is it enough

walking a long road
persevering misfortune

lonely water
the moon
a seed

this is what you forget
that we don't want the fallen sun

every straight line is true

tell me with surprise
in the cold morning

the people
the earth

the snow

   so barren
so dark

25

You can never give enough
 to repay what you owe.
For this reason, she is held
 to have said:

I am the song and
I am the silence

I am what you must learn and
I am what no one can teach.

26

My son, does anyone want to be a slave?
To sit with their back to the mysteries,
to long for more simple answers, never asking
why the star always pierces
their eye, but never anyone else's,
eager to be left out of the negotiations
because peace is for everyone else, not them?

27

The sand, fleeing the sky, whispers
against you, praying for help.
You will not help.

Hands to the sun, you will pray
for help. The sun will not help.

The sun will turn to the night,
and try to burn it.
The night will not burn.

The night will smother the sky,
smother the sun, smother you,
smother the sand.

Indeed even the smallest ones
never listen to prayers they believe
are fake.

28

It is your custom:
Refuse everything.
Teach nothing.
Bolt your doors every night.
And say to yourselves:
*When will they come
and take back what is theirs?*

29

Will you wait for the dust
    to tell you what you want to say?
Will you wait for the star
    to come around at last?
Will you wait to find a way
    to keep from weeping?
Will you wait to comfort
    yourself, to comfort each other?
Blessed are you who weep
    and who are oppressed
    by those without hope.

30

To lie down in the water to see
what the clouds can teach you.

To walk away to see
what you cannot leave behind.

This is not the beginning of death
but the beginning of wisdom.

every generation trying to change the end
the sunset in my own voice so cruel
nowhere instead I will ask ancestors
at dawn to follow tomorrow's door

day is always fading
but he will listen
to the color of the sky
like a word

it is good beneath the sun
beyond the slow night
abandoned as the day began
as yellow as winter

        nothing
      nothing
  late

     new world
   the tall blue sky
in the green country

31

What passes for drink
on this parched and transient
steppe will have to satisfy
you, or you will never find rest.

You worry at your destiny
without a thought to the root
that holds you where you
stay. You cannot simply sever
it like a hair. You cannot
simply ride away
before a train of dust.

This mean and abashed
outpost, which will soon
be erased like hoofmarks
after the spring floods, was
once a metropolis, always
above you like the sun.
But the sun will set.

32

And you sit behind the green
flash, but the day
of your light remains.

And you sit as you always do,
sand like nursery rhymes
running through your fingers,
as you give yourself over
to the new moon.

33

With a syllable that
struck you like a long
expected blow, or an argument
that lingered like
a penitential fast, you have
come to know the Son
of Man. And not just
in the cloud beneath you,
but in your head
which you strive to pull off
like a dandelion—that is:
you have come know yourself.

34

And you wear your repose
    like a mask, as though
    you had neither envy
    nor groaning nor death
    within you.

And you travel
    a thousand miles
    without moving a foot
    beyond your sanctuary.

And you have nowhere left
    to go, neither the red
    house nor the white hill.

35

And how easy to say, *Release yourself*
from every bond so that you may bloom
into freedom. But what does this
really mean? You must hold your hand
in a fire without burning. You must draw
a tooth from your jaw. You must fly
before you can crawl. You must turn
the weather aside. You must go
blindly into a forest of razors.

36

And you could look out
over the falling mountain,
shy beneath its green
rivers and fanning itself
with the green sunrises.
Motionless as it counted
every leaf, and counted
every leaf again.

And what would you say?
And what would you see?
And the luminous was hidden.

good comes from wonder
like a luminous place
the wind reading waiting
the air is everything

I will sing but will not wait
you slowly look around
mean small cruel
you already fight

> *stories*
> *colors*
smoke
> *skin*

I asked him nothing else
> *it is*
> *it is*
impossible

no matter how many times

catching a handful of small seeds

> *on your arm*
> *on your knee*
under its road

hesitant dream

37

Every fish sings of this,
how the round queen, who gathers
the sleepless rain and holds it fast
again and again, became dark
because her consort would not
agree with her. Then slowly
she turned and sent
the rising waters back to him.

38

On the first day of the new
custom, when they show
that they are abetting
the world, one foot on water
and one on land, they
cannot know how habit
will erase them, leaving them
to swim endlessly toward
an unreachable shore. And
they will long for the light, and
they will turn away from the light.

39

They tell you
that peace is nothing
like fire,
that they swim
in the light of truth,
that they float
in their ancient customs
that guide them
along the fine edge between
love and terror.

But they are not
acquainted with the origin
of chaos, nor with
its root, which grows
in the light of
love and terror.

40

Twice a day,
they trip over
the fine ribbon
that lies between
night and day.

They cannot guess
what is hiding
behind the color
yellow. They ask
for help by
closing their eyes.

Their skin knows
this better than
they do: it
is in light
that light exists.

It is obvious,
and I don't
need to say
it again: almost
no one knows
their own soul.

41

I will not give you
what you ask for.
I will dog your heel
as you forage for your
herbs in the round garden.

As the soil gives way
to sand, there will be
days when you will
look for me, and you
will not find me.

42

I am the mouth and
I am the cry

I am the pavement you lie on and
I am the knee that holds you there

I am the blood and
I am the ear that listens to the blood

I am the one who stands and
I am the one who runs

I am the liberator and
I am the one bound to the stake

I am forgiveness and vendetta
I am the judgment and the acquittal.

And whenever you hide, I will appear.

river
lake
clouds
roots
seeds
road
fire
blood
law
time
sky
mountains
earth
singing
restless

you give too late
their secrets know the way

choice
confusion
order
the winds
the moon
the path

up   up

this muddy path is waiting
for its new name

hollow branches around the mysteries

43

He could eat with them
when he returned.

He didn't seem to know
what had transpired
while he was gone.

He appeared
to the small as small,
to the angels as an angel,
and to men as a man.

He spoke of a mountain.

When asked, *What is good?*
he said, *The cold.*

After he departed again,
nothing
made sense to them
anymore.

44

Can you touch
what is false?
Can you know
your own heart?
Is it good?
Does it orbit
a star? Will
you let it
teach you anything?
On the contrary!
You dwell in
darkness. And, full
of bitterness, you
are drunk with
the empty fire.

45

The everywhere of now, he says,
this red willow, this nightfall
of starlings. They throw their black
song like a net to catch stray
voices. Split a piece of wood, he says,

and I am there. My breath
turns blood red then black.
This is how you can know
I am here. And when I am not here,
he says, lift up the stone

and you will find me.

46

what do they want
this fear like an egg
this panic like a dead fish

what do they want
their temples mere tumbles
of hot bricks their uncovered
heads open to the sky

what do they want
they shake their heads
at the stubborn sun

what do they want
so pious and they cannot
keep their law it works only
with the engine of heresy
the drought of jealousy
what more do they want

47

We watched them, standing
near the fire. We could
hear them whisper of
who they would kill

next. And I asked, they
who did not know but
have turned away:
where will their souls go?

But I was alone, and the
moon said nothing.

48

When you are seized
by the small terror
of the endless stones
pressing down upon you
and you undergo these sufferings
and peace leaves you
breathless and the way
is blocked by a multitude
jeering and refusing to help,

only the sun will stand
by you, holding out
its shy hand
to lead you home.

Four Lessons

Through the gift of the spirit
the four lights appeared.
What does this mean,
"through the gift"?
It means help is always
near but not always near
enough. What does this
mean, "of the spirit"?
It means what is true
is always true but not
always true enough.
What does this mean,
"the four lights"? It means
it is always day even when we
are trapped deep within
the earth. What does this
mean, "appeared"? It means
even the mutable is fixed,
like a leaf always withering
and always unfolding.

Afterword

The poems in this book come from a time when I didn't think I was writing anything. Each day, I dutifully coaxed myself to the blank page, which all too often remained blank. Each day was folded over on itself, false and empty.

So I turned to a variety of language games and bibliomancies—opening dictionaries at random, listening to several podcasts and TV shows at once and picking out words as they went past, and so on. I finally settled on something called the "Ten Minute Spill" by Rita Dove, which I had found in *The Practice of Poetry*, edited by Robin Behn and Chase Twichell. Here's how it goes: With ten minutes on the clock, write a ten-line poem using five words from a predetermined list and an adage or idiomatic phrase (e.g. *a stitch in time saves nine; a needle in a haystack*). And that's it. Don't try anything fancy: no rhyming or meter of any sort. Just spend ten minutes figuring out how to pepper the words and the adage over the course of ten lines into something resembling a poem or poem-like thing. How long is each line? Doesn't matter! Is it even a poem? Who cares!

In my more or less daily variation, I kept the time and line constraint, but I decided to pick the words and the adage randomly, through chance operations. I collected a very long numbered list of words and rolled my old D&D dice to pick the five words. Instead of an adage, I chose a line at random from a book. I never looked back at the previous days' poems or began revising and editing them until I had accumulated at least thirty or forty and was ready to reshuffle the word-list and move to a new book to serve as the source text.

Choosing a source text was one of the more difficult parts of the project. At first, I tried to avoid any books which were already personally significant to me. I remembered how Tom Phillips had chosen the book for the project that would become *A Humument*. His sole criterion: "the first (coherent) book I could find for threepence would serve." Several of my own source texts were, therefore, chosen randomly using the same sorts of chance operations I was using to assemble the recipes for the poems. Curiously, of the six or seven different books I used, the only three that rendered anything fruitful were ones that I did, in fact, have very intense relationships with.

For the poems in "This Folded Path," I threw the *I Ching*, taking images from the trigrams or phrases from the Judgment. For "This False Life," I chose a line at random from the NYRB edition of Thoreau's *Journal.* The date at the beginning of each poem is the journal entry from which the sentence was drawn. And for "This Empty Tongue," I turned to the *Nag Hammadi Library*, a collection of Gnostic writings and non-canonical gospels unearthed in 1945.

Once all the poems had been finished, I fired them in the kiln and arranged them on their shelves. Then I took them down again and shattered them on the floor, building new poems from the shards. The poems that appear within Parts I and II are built from fragments of Part III, and those in Part III from fragments of Parts I and II.

The point of all this randomness, all these chance operations, all these games with coins and dice, was to leave as much of the decision-making process until the very moment I began composing. I was too swamped by the quotidian to hear anything else; if I allowed myself to pick the words, I knew they would be nothing but *fear, mask, Covid, police, murder, Covid, racist, protest, climate, rage, rage, rage*—and that's what most of each day already was. The chance operations led me away from the unhealthy polarity of either willfully ignoring the appalling spectacle or being angrily transfixed by it. Instead, I entered a third space beyond this polarity. I knew the worries, rages, and sorrows of those pandemic years would find their way into the poems anyway. They always do, of course, because poems are

144

part of the world, and the world is part of every poem. But this way, they arrived obliquely, as I listened for different sounds and invited the shy sparks in my peripheral vision to wander out into the room. And for ten minutes each day, I remembered that, as Thoreau said, "Thank Heaven, here is not all the world."

Acknowledgments

This book was composed during a time of disquiet, isolation, and absences, when no amount of support would have seemed sufficient. So, I am grateful for the friendships that have sustained me over the years, and often over great distances, in this life of poetry: Kate MacVean, Richard Jeffrey Newman, Victor Gonzales, Andrew Greenberg, and the inimitable Anne Klus. I am grateful to the memory of my poetry teachers: Wes Schultz and the poet John Engman. Thanks also to early supporters of the book, who understood it long before I did: Eileen R. Tabios, Mark Young, Patrick Pritchett, Mark Scroggins, Claire Wahmanholm, and Henry Gould.

Grateful acknowledgment to Jane Huffman at Guesthouse Lit, where "Four Lessons" first appeared, and to the relentless rob mclennan of above/ground press for issuing a version of part one as a chapbook. Thanks especially to Unsolicited Press for selecting this book for publication.

But most of all, I am grateful for the patience, strength, and wisdom of my wife, Ana Morel, without whom this book, my writing, and indeed my life, would be far poorer.

About the Author

Robert van Vliet grew up in the Twin Cities and spent many years living in lots of other places. He has been, among other things, a process manager, a singer/songwriter, a repair technician for Macintosh computers, and a typographer. His poetry has appeared in *The Sixth Chamber Review, Autumn Sky Poetry Daily, Wine Cellar Press, Otoliths,* and elsewhere. He lives and teaches in Saint Paul, Minnesota.

About Unsolicited Press

Unsolicited Press is based out of Portland, Oregon and focuses on the works of the unsung and underrepresented. As a womxn-owned, all-volunteer small publisher that doesn't worry about profits as much as championing exceptional literature, we have the privilege of partnering with authors skirting the fringes of the lit world. We've worked with emerging and award-winning authors such as Shann Ray, Amy Shimshon-Santo, Brook Bhagat, Kris Amos, and John W. Bateman.

Learn more at unsolicitedpress.com. Find us on twitter and instagram.